The End of a Nation

Studies in the book of Obadiah

Paul Young

© 2002 Paul Young
ISBN 0-9523478-4-9

Published in Great Britain.

All rights reserved.

No part of this publication may be reproduced or transmitted, in any form by any means, electronic or mechanical, including photocopying, recording, or any information storage and retrieval system, without permission in writing.

Printed by:
Bible Studies Institute,
Lower Glenageary Road, Dun Loaghaire, Co. Dublin, Ireland

Foreword

This small book on the prophecy of Obadiah was first preached in young people's rallies in the city of Cardiff in South Wales. I confess that I had never until that time heard of Obadiah being preached and so it was breaking new ground in my ministry. Those messages were thoroughly revised and formed a series of radio broadcasts for the Trans World Radio programme 'Truth for Today'. They are now given a more permanent format, which we trust and pray will prove a rich blessing to those who love to study the Word of God.

In some ways the book can be viewed almost as an allegory of the warfare, which every Christian experiences between the 'flesh' (pictured as Edom in the prophecy) and the 'spirit' (pictured as Jacob in the prophecy). There is undoubtedly much validity to such an approach. However, I have taken the text within its historical, geographical and political setting and have drawn out the spiritual lessons, which I trust, will be helpful to those who read this book.

My thanks to Eric Davies and his missionary helper Penny for all their hard work in bringing this book to completion.

Paul Young

Contents

Foreward

Obadiah 1a · 7

Obadiah 1 - 4 · 15

Obadiah 5 - 9 · 23

Obadiah 3a · 31

Obadiah 10 -14 · · · · · · · · · · · · · · · · · · · 39

Obadiah 15 - 16 · · · · · · · · · · · · · · · · · · 47

Obadiah 17 - 18 · · · · · · · · · · · · · · · · · · 55

Obadiah 19 - 21 · · · · · · · · · · · · · · · · · · 63

The Book of Obadiah

Reading: Obadiah 1a

"The vision of Obadiah."

This fascinating book known to us as 'Obadiah' is the shortest of all the thirty-nine books found in the Old Testament. In our English Bible it is just twenty-one verses in length and takes just a few minutes to read. It is easy to miss it and to by-pass its message, but that would be a serious mistake, because it has a vital message for us today, even in the twenty-first century. One commentator writing about the book of Obadiah said, "It is not quoted in the New Testament, yet its message is a vital part of all the prophetic Scriptures. It is written in lucid and forceful language." While another writer has described the prophecy as, "this remarkable fragment from the pen of Obadiah".

A fragment it may be, taking only a moment or two to read but it takes much longer to get to grips with its message and understand what God is saying through His servant. It takes even longer to learn its lessons in a practical way and submit to its teaching in humble obedience. Yet this must always be the aim of our Bible reading to be instructed in the ways of God and surrender to His will and live lives of Christlikeness. If we lose sight of this aim, then we lose sight of the very reason that we as Christians read and study our Bibles.

The Author

The writer of this book is named 'Obadiah'. He is really a very obscure person, about whom we know very little, as one commentator has written, "Of Obadiah himself nothing is known. Not even his father's name is given in the title of the book." So we don't know from which town he originated, though we do know from reading the prophecy,

The End of a Nation

that he conducted his ministry in the Southern Kingdom of Judah. We have no idea who his family were and know nothing about his background. We are ignorant about his secular occupation, or indeed if he had one at all and we have no indication of his personal appearance. We can seriously ask the question, "Who was Obadiah?" and we cannot find the answer, but certainly the name was a common one in Israel and this seen in the fact that twelve people in the Old Testament carry the name 'Obadiah'.

The point, however, is clearly made that the messenger is not important but his message is of vital importance. The focus of attention is not on the prophet but on his prophecy. This should always be the case with every servant of God. Our aim is to bring God's message to the people and there is no room for self-glory or for building up a personal following. The attitude of John the Baptist towards Christ seemed to characterise Obadiah and should be seen in every follower of the Saviour. John said, "He must increase, but I must decrease." (*John 3.30*). Or as a hymn writer put it, "That I am nothing, Thou art all. I would be daily taught." This was also the attitude described by the Apostle Paul when he wrote in Philippians, "Let nothing be done through strife or vainglory; but in lowliness of mind let each esteem other better than themselves." (*Philippians 2.3*). So we are called not to look at Obadiah, but to grasp and take in the message of God through Obadiah. The brevity of the book must not put us off as if shortness meant insignificance. Clearly when vital issues are at stake, words are not to be wasted and each one of the words in this book is of real significance.

The meaning of the name 'Obadiah' carries two ideas. The first is 'Worshipper of Jehovah' and the second is 'Servant of Jehovah'. There is not a great deal of difference between these two concepts, because it is impossible to worship God if we fail to serve Him and

The Book of Obadiah

equally we can't truly serve Him, if we fail to worship Him. Both imply a deep love for God, a real obedience to God and a focus upon the glory of God. To truly serve and worship God requires a commitment of everything about us, all surrendered to His will. This is the normal expectation for every Christian and is summarised in the words of a famous hymn:

> 'All to Jesus I surrender, all to Him I freely give.
> I will ever love and trust Him, in his presence daily live.
> I surrender all. I surrender all. All to thee my blessed Saviour,
> I surrender all.'

Obadiah is at pains to emphasise that his message derived from the Lord. It is described as 'the vision' (*v.1*). A vision is a sort of daytime dream and implies that he received his message from God in the form of a vision. God spoke to his servant in that vision and gave him the prophecy that he would subsequently proclaim and eventually was incorporated into the inspired Holy Scriptures. A vision also implies seeing. Obadiah saw in a vision the Lord who gave him his message or he saw the outworking of his vision as a sort of panorama in his mind. It must have been awesome, and he was deeply aware that the message was not his own but that of the Lord's. This fact he makes clear when he writes the following statements:

"This is what the Sovereign Lord says…" (*v.1*)

"…declares the Lord" (*v.4*)

"…declares the Lord" (*v.8*)

"The Lord has spoken." (*v.18*)

So Obadiah makes it very plain that he was not the author of the

The End of a Nation

message, but that it came directly from the Lord. The implication seems to be that if you disagree with the message, then your argument is not with Obadiah, for he is just the messenger, but with the Lord who is the author and originator of that message. That is the same today whenever the Gospel of Jesus Christ is presented. People may react against the message, but their reaction is really against God who formulated that Gospel as the only answer to mankind's deepest need.

The Message of Obadiah

The prophecy can be summarised as 'judgement upon the nation of Edom', though in the closing verses there is also emphasis upon the salvation of Israel. The main thrust of this prophecy is directed towards Edom and so we need to remind ourselves about this long-forgotten people. These People, known as Edomites, featured prominently on many of the pages of the Old Testament, but have disappeared from the world of nations, obliterated through the course of history.

The name 'Edom' means 'red' and was a sort of nickname that was given to Jacob's twin brother Esau. He received this nickname when he sold his birthright to Jacob for a bowl of red stew (***Genesis 25.30***). Also the name may have been the result of the fact that Esau was red haired (***Genesis 25.25***) or that the land his descendants inhabited was a country with red soil. The descendants of Esau became known as the nation of Edom and they inhabited the region to the south and east of the Dead Sea, which stretched southward as far as the tip of the northeastern arm of the Red Sea. It was a mountainous land that made it easily defendable and also it was on trade routes that enabled it to exact tolls upon travellers. The area inhabited by Edom was also

The Book of Obadiah

known as Mount Seir, as the book of Genesis makes clear, "So Esau (that is, Edom) settled in the hill country of Seir...Esau the father of the Edomites." (***Genesis 36.8-9***). Yet Mount Seir was not just one mountain but a mountainous region and Obadiah draws attention to this in his prophecy.

In King David's time the land of Edom had been conquered by Israel and in Solomon's reign the Edomite port of Ezion-geber was used to launch ocean going vessels to trade and bring back wealth for the nation of Israel and the king's court in Jerusalem. When Israel's military prowess weakened Edom gained its independence and as Obadiah relates in this book was delighted when the Babylonian armies overran Jerusalem.

However, eventually Edom, as foretold by the Hebrew prophets was itself overrun and destroyed. This was many years after Obadiah's time. The destruction led to groups of Edomites travelling west and finding refuge and safety around the town of Hebron. The area became known as Idumea and was eventually conquered by the Roman armies and incorporated into the Roman Empire. One of those Idumeans was a man who is known today as Herod the Great. He was appointed king of Palestine by the Romans and was a man of great energy and organising ability. He built forts and defensive structures and organised his army and is infamous for the fact that he killed the infants in and around Bethlehem in an abortive attempt to kill the infant Christ.

Thus Edom was really a brother nation to Israel. The two sons of Isaac were fathers of these two nations. The people of Edom were descendants of Esau and the people of Israel were descendants from Jacob. Indeed ***v.10*** of Obadiah reminds Edom of this sibling connection with the words, "your brother Jacob". So the two countries

The End of a Nation

were really brother nations and should have been friendly towards each other, as they had descended from common ancestral stock. Instead they were bitter enemies and this was not the friendly rivalry or jostling for position often associated with siblings. Instead it was a bitter rivalry for power, wealth and influence and in this prophecy Edom is seen to be at fault and Obadiah predicts God's judgement upon them as a nation. He states in clear and unmistakable terms their final doom and utter annihilation as a nation.

Obviously the prophecy came true and the nation of Edom is no longer. There is no representation of such a country in the United Nations and no flag is raised in the name of Edom. The country ceased to exist, its cities and dwellings lie empty and decaying and its people are unheard of today. God's words are never uttered in vain and as He foretells the events of the future, we should never doubt that they will most definitely come to pass. We live in a time when the prophetic statements of God, especially in relation to the Second Coming of Christ, are seriously doubted and even denied with mocking scorn by many people. Obadiah's words and the subsequent history of Edom should stand, as a powerful reminder that the Word of the Lord endures forever and none of His promises will fail.

The Reasons for Judgement upon Edom

The message of God concerning Edom's destruction was due to two factors. These two reasons may seem to the twenty-first century Western mind as insufficient for such judgement, but we must remember that God's ways are according to righteousness and He will destroy sin and the injustice and inequality caused by selfishness. It is therefore a severe warning to us. The two reasons for judgement are as follows.

The Book of Obadiah

Firstly, there was the pride or arrogance displayed by Edom, especially towards Israel, but ultimately towards God. Pride is an inward attitude, essentially a state of mind, which views the world from the standpoint of self-centred self-sufficiency. It is one of the most awful sins and is roundly and soundly condemned in Scripture. In the book of ***Proverbs*** we read that, "Pride goes before destruction and a haughty spirit before a fall" (***16.18***) and that is a summary of the attitude and experience of Edom. We also read in ***Proverbs*** these words, "Pride and arrogancy…do I hate." (***8.13***) Thus we see that God hates pride and the arrogant spirit and this is because it is a spiritually fatal sin. It can ruin personal lives, church life and bring division, hurt and deep wounds to the human spirit.

God has called his people to humbleness and not pride. However, humbleness must not be confused with inferiority. The Christian must not consider himself as inferior and so develop a complex. The Christian is willing to do any work the Lord calls him to perform, but recognises that without the help of the Lord he can never achieve success in that work. That is why the apostle wrote, "I can do all things through Christ who strengthens me." (***Philippians 4.13***)

The second sin of Edom was violence and intense cruelty towards Israel. This was attitude displayed in action. This was the outward manifestation of the inward feelings. Edom was exploitative and bitter in their unjust and evil behaviour towards Israel. They compounded the troubles that Israel was going through and showed not one ounce of human compassion, pity or kindness. Theirs was a compounded evil directed at the people of God.

There is nothing new under the sun and the church of God has often found itself the object of hatred and persecution. This was true in the time of Acts when Stephen was stoned to death and the apostle James

The End of a Nation

was killed with the sword, while others were beaten, imprisoned, threatened and deported. It is still true today in many circumstances and situations. Jesus knew what was coming and warned, "If they have persecuted me they will persecute you." (***John 15.20***) The apostle Paul wrote, "All that will live godly in Christ Jesus shall suffer persecution." (***2 Tim. 3.12***) So such treatment is not unusual and must not take the people of God by surprise.

So we see that Edom was condemned for their inner attitude and their outward actions. What we are inwardly will always affect what we do outwardly. We sow a thought we reap an action. It is true that character and conduct are very closely linked. That's why the teaching of the Lord Jesus in the Sermon on the Mount emphasised both the inward, namely what we are, as well as the outward what we do. God is concerned for both and so we must maintain a cleanness and holiness in our hearts and minds, through prayer, Bible reading and focusing our attention on what is clean, good and wholesome. This will lead to cleanness and holiness in daily conduct and we will then live lives that glorify the name of Christ and bring blessing to those we come in contact with day by day.

The Book of Obadiah

Reading: Obadiah 1-4

"The vision of Obadiah. Thus says the Lord God concerning Edom (we have heard a report from the LORD, And a messenger has been sent among the nations, saying, "Arise, and let us rise up against her for battle"): "Behold, I will make you small among the nations; You shall be greatly despised. The pride of your heart has deceived you. You who dwell in the clefts of the rock, Whose habitation is high: You who say in your heart, 'Who will bring me down to the ground?' Though you exalt yourself as high as the eagle, And though you set your nest among the stars, From there I will bring you down," says the LORD"

The message of Obadiah is a message predicting judgement and punishment from the Lord upon the nation of Edom. Edom was condemned for its pride and its violent behaviour. Thus God condemned both inward attitude and outward actions, each are important and we should take such warnings to heart.

As Obadiah gave his prophecy it is clear that Edom's doom and destruction had already been determined by the direct will of God. Obadiah, with others, had heard 'a message from the Lord', we know that others were involved because he uses the plural word "we" in the first verse. Clearly Obadiah was not the only prophet through whom this message came, others had also heard the news. An obvious example was the prophet Jeremiah who had also received a message, "concerning Edom" (*49.7*) and perhaps Obadiah is quoting from that prophecy, or perhaps they both heard from a common source, ultimately from the Lord Himself. So Obadiah is not a lone voice bringing the sad news of Edom's demise, others too had received similar messages from God.

The End of a Nation

God's Method of Judgement

The Lord's chosen method of executing judgement upon Edom was to bring invading armies to attack and destroy them as a nation. So an envoy or ambassador, otherwise known as a messenger had been sent to the nations calling them to rise up in battle against Edom. It is unclear who exactly could have been that messenger to the nations. Indeed it may not have been any particular person, but a feeling, a spirit amongst the nations that made them feel antagonistic towards Edom. The true source of that stirring up of the nations was the Lord. The word "nations" is translated in the Authorised Version as "heathen" and refers to non-Jewish peoples.

The envoy to the nations brings one simple message that becomes the battle cry of these people. "Rise, and let us go against her for battle" (v.1). This is the Lord stirring up the emotions of nations and their leaders to see Edom as an enemy. To be antagonistic towards the descendants of Esau and to insist upon inflicting punishment upon that nation who inhabited the areas to the east and south of the Dead Sea. Subsequently, various nations attacked and invaded the mountain strongholds of Edom. These included the Assyrians, then Nebuchadnezzar and his Babylonian-lead confederation of nations. Eventually Edom was fully subdued under the Romans and lost its national identity and existence forever.

The Results of God's Judgement

In *v.2* God speaks directly to Edom through the prophet Obadiah and two important statements are made concerning the nation's future. Firstly, it will be made "small among the nations". Of course, Edom had never been an empire-building people. They inhabited a small and

The Book of Obadiah

insignificant tract of land in the Middle East and had never expanded their borders to conquer or invade other tribes of people and bring them under their control. Yet in the future Edom would be even smaller, even more insignificant, a nation so obscure as to be non-existent. How true that prophetic statement was. Edom is no longer and has not been in existence for hundreds of years.

Secondly, God says to Edom, "you will be utterly despised". At the time of Obadiah Edom was experiencing a period of prosperity and strength. It had high standing in the community of nations, but says God that will eventually be changed. Through successive invasions, the nation will be so weakened that it will be considered weak, ineffective and poor. It will be unable to stand up for itself and its glory and prosperity will fade until it is a despised outcast. At that point it will be a complete irrelevance in the military, political and commercial world of the Middle East. They would be just an impotent people totally at the mercy of others.

These will be the results of judgement upon Edom.

The Reasons for God's Judgement

The essential reason for the forthcoming judgement upon the nation was its pride. It was a proud and arrogant people. They felt important, powerful and impregnable. They gloried and boasted in their strength and wealth. However, pride is very deceitful. Indeed God says to Edom, "The pride of your heart has deceived you." (*v.3*). We must be careful that we are not deceived by our proud attitude. Pride is deceptive in a number of ways.

Firstly, it stops us trusting in the Lord. It is an attitude of self-sufficiency, that seeks the answers to our problems and needs

The End of a Nation

within ourselves. It refuses to seek for those answers outside of ourselves by looking up to the Lord. It is the attempt to deal with things in our own strength, with our own resources, with our own plans and ideas. This is the heart of the person who refuses the free salvation that is offered in Christ. It is the insistence that we have something to do in the achievement of our place in Heaven.

This essentially is the basis of false religion that seems to think that we can achieve acceptance with God through observing rules, regulations and rituals. That if we work hard enough we will reach the standard that God requires and will be able to enter Heaven. If such an approach were true then we would have achieved our own salvation and would be able to boast and take pride in what we had accomplished. However, the New Testament is most insistent upon the fact that we can never reach God's standard for entry into His presence. We must rely upon His provision and His provision alone for our eternal salvation. That provision was His Son, Jesus Christ and His vital work of atonement at Calvary's cross. The Apostle Paul put it this way:

"For it is by grace you have been saved, through faith – and that not from yourselves, it is the gift of God – not by works, so that no-one can boast." (***Ephesians 2.8-9***)

So it is faith and faith alone, that brings salvation. As we learn to trust in the Lord Jesus we receive forgiveness, cleansing from sin and eternal life. What a wonderful joy, what a great blessing, what a genuine relief that is. It is not the result of what I have done but in whom I have believed that counts with God and that stands sure for the whole of eternity.

So the first problem caused by pride is that it stops us trusting in God.

The Book of Obadiah

Secondly, it stops us caring for others. Pride focuses upon self and upon our personal needs. It is consumed and preoccupied with personal need and doesn't have time to be concerned for the needs of others, so these can all too easily be ignored. Pride finds excuses to avoid the inconvenience and disruption to daily routine that helping those who are in need would entail.

A number of years ago a tramp, filthy and dirty, slept overnight on the front doorstep of a church building. He was still there the next day when the people came to worship. He was told in no uncertain terms to 'get up' and leave. He slowly got up, picked up his rags and few belongings, put them in a shopping trolley and moved away. One of the church attenders said, "We don't want his type around here!" Someone else got a bucket of water and disinfectant and washed the front doorstep. The shame was that no help or compassion was shown towards that destitute man. It was beneath the dignity of those people to help him. I know it would be costly to help him, because he was so dirty and smelt abominably. He may not have been thankful for any assistance. Pride condemned that man and offered no help. Humility would have offered assistance and reached out to him in love.

In contrast a church group were meeting for a week of fellowship and relaxation at a hotel complex. Each evening they had a time of hymn singing and Bible teaching. It was a rich and fulfilling time of sharing and blessing. One evening a little girl was sick and burst into tears at the disruption she had caused. Her parents were obviously embarrassed. Yet with no second thought two elders of that church got down on hands and knees and cleared up the mess. It was not beneath their dignity to help and care for that little family group. It made a big impact and in the testimonies at the end of the week a number spoke of the reality of Christian love shown by the leaders who were not too proud to help clear up a mess created by a very sick little girl.

The End of a Nation

How sad it is when pride stops people caring for the needs of others. This is the second problem that is engendered by an arrogant attitude. The nation of Edom certainly saw no need to trust in the true and living God and thought they could prosper by their own efforts. They also saw no need to help other nations in need, especially not, their brother nation, Israel who at that time was in the most desperate of straits through foreign invasion and cruelty.

The Basis for Edom's Pride

The people of Edom felt secure because they lived in mountain fortresses. These were often cut into the very rock faces of the cliffs. So their defensive points were surrounded by very steep slopes and could only be reached by extremely narrow passes through the rocky mountainous terrain. The most famous such fortress was the ancient Edomite City of Petra (which was also known as 'Sela'). Today it is a great tourist attraction in Jordan and can be approached only through those steep canyons. It is uninhabited and is known as 'the silent city of the forgotten past'. Such cities could easily be defended from invading armies. The advantage always appeared to be with the defenders rather than the attackers and so Edom felt that their position was impregnable and that they could never be defeated or their defensive positions over run by an invading army. How wrong they were!

Thus Obadiah was not exaggerating when he described Edom as living "in the clefts of the rocks" and "who make your home on the heights" (*v.3*). Those high fortresses gave Edom a sense of security and they gloated and boasted, "Who can bring me down to the ground?" They felt that no army on earth could successfully invade and overrun their mountain strongholds. Thus they saw no need to ask for assistance from God or from any other nation. They were self-sufficient and proud of their seemingly impregnable position. As a nation they were

The Book of Obadiah

in for a shock and must have wondered at the words that Obadiah addressed to them so directly.

So Edom believed that no one could remove them from their mountain strongholds. Yet there was one who could do it and who would do it and that was God. He says to them that even if their fortresses were higher, they would not be too high for Him to deal with them. In *v. 4* the description is given of Edom being as high as where eagle's soar. This is difficult to understand and maybe it means that even if Edom's fortresses were in the most inaccessible places where only eagles could build their nests God could bring them down. Maybe it is more figurative and means that if the stronghold was in the sky, where only clouds and birds are seen, it is not too high for God to reach. This latter view is reinforced by the fact that the challenge is further developed with the words, "and make your nest among the stars". No one can actually make their home amongst the stars and this is a picture for the most exalted and secure place it is possible for man to imagine.

Yet even in such a place of seeming total security, it is not out of reach of the Lord. There can be no hiding place from Almighty God. In fact the prophet Jeremiah makes this very point when he wrote:

"Can any hide himself in secret places that I shall not see him? saith the Lord. Do not I fill heaven and earth? saith the Lord." (*Jeremiah 23.24*)

There is no place in Heaven or earth that is secure from the probing eyes of the Lord. He is the one who is omnipotent and no defensive structure is able to withstand His almighty power. So with utter assurance, Edom's question, "Who can bring me down to the ground?" is answered, "I will bring you down, says the Lord". Thus the arrogance of Edom will be dealt with and the boasting of the descendants of Esau will be stopped.

The End of a Nation

Today many people have defied God and think that all is well. They may deny His very existence, deny His coming judgement upon sinners, and deny the possibility of punishment for sin. They may deride His Word and mock the simple faith of the ordinary Christian believer. Such arrogant strongholds of the heart and mind will be brought low, because as the Apostle Paul wrote:

"At the name of Jesus every knee shall bow, in heaven and on earth and under the earth, and every tongue confess that Jesus Christ is Lord, to the glory of God the Father." (***Philippians 2.10,11***)

The true Christian has already found the stronghold of his heart breached by the saving grace of the Lord Jesus. The true Christian has recognised the inner need for forgiveness and cleansing from sin. He has turned to the Lord in repentance and faith and acknowledged that need. He has realised that the only possible way to be saved is through faith in the one who loved him, died on the cross for his sin and who was raised to life again on the third day. Thus in an act of commitment to Christ he believed and received him as Saviour. The deep desire of the true Christian is to serve the Lord Jesus for the rest of his life.

If pride fills your heart like the hearts of the Edomites, now is the time to confess such sin and reach for God's forgiveness. Humbly seek the Lord and in due time He will exalt you into the wonder and glory of Heaven.

What a wonderful message Obadiah has and how powerfully relevant it is as a message for men and women in the twenty-first century.

The Book of Obadiah

Reading: Obadiah 5-9

"If thieves had come to you, If robbers by night – Oh, how you will be cut off! – Would they not have stolen till they had enough? If grape-gatherers had come to you, Would they not have left some gleanings? Oh, how Esau shall be searched out! How his hidden treasures shall be sought after! All the men in your confederacy shall force you to the border, the men at peace with you shall deceive you and prevail against you. Those who eat bread shall lay a trap for you. No one is aware of it. 'Will I not in that day,' says the LORD, 'Even destroy the wise men from Edom, and understanding from the mountains of Esau?' Then your mighty men, O Teman, shall be dismayed, to the end that everyone from the mountain of Esau may be cut off by slaughter."

Obadiah's message is a pronouncement of coming judgement upon the nation of Edom. He outlined with graphic detail the ultimate fate of the nation and the reason for God's punishment. Essentially Edom had been arrogant and violent, inward attitude and outward action that the Lord found extremely distasteful.

In these verses we see some of the causes for this judgement and some of the effects of the judgement. We see the root and the fruit, as clearly Edom reaped the consequences of what it, as a nation, had sown. In earlier verses we noticed that Edom had the most amazing military defences. Their fortresses were cut into the high rock faces and humanly speaking they seemed impregnable. Yet the Lord clearly stated that He would bring them down and the nation would be defeated. However, Edom had other aspects of its national life in which to glory and boast and that led to the nation becoming an arrogant people.

The End of a Nation

Edom's Great Wealth

The nation of Edom was not an impoverished people, indeed they had great wealth. Much of their riches were derived from their geographical position. Firstly, they were on trade routes. The 'Eastern Highway' went through their region and they were able to extract tolls and tariffs from merchants and traders who used that route. Secondly, they were great producers of copper and were able to sell their products for considerable profit. It all added up to a people who gloried in their riches.

It is an interesting fact that Jesus talked of the difficulty, the almost impossibility of rich people entering into the kingdom of God. He said, "It is easier for a camel to go through the eye of a needle, than for a rich man to enter into the kingdom of God". (***Mark 10.25***) Some have said that 'the eye of a needle' refers to a low city gate and for a camel to go through it; it has to shed its load and kneel down. They say that this represents man having to 'forsake all' and bow before the Lordship of Christ. However, the disciples, at the time Jesus said those words, didn't seem to see it quite like that and thought it was impossible for someone to go through a needle's eye, and of course it is impossible, "but not with God: for with God all things are possible". (***Mark 10.27***)

The problem with wealth is that it is too easy for us to allow it to become our master, instead of keeping it as our servant. Money is necessary, especially in contemporary society, but the love of money is the root of many kinds of evil. Money makes us materially comfortable, but it can blind our minds to the deeper spiritual needs of the soul. Many have viewed abundant material resources as a curse, because there is always the desperate necessity to protect those resources and build upon them. Also those vital intangible qualities of life, that cannot be quantified in terms of price are often derided and

The Book of Obadiah

denigrated in a materialistic society. So friendship, love, relationships, joy, contentment and concern for others are in much shorter supply in the affluent societies of the world.

Thus the message of the Gospel with its emphasis upon self-denial, sacrifice and care for others is often ignored and despised in a self-indulgent, hedonistic community where money is the dominating and motivating force.

Edom was a moneymaking community and was doing well financially and that made them despise others, with an uncaring attitude. They also saw no need to trust the Lord, as they had all sorts of "hidden treasures" as *v.6* makes clear. Yet that wealth would be dissipated and Obadiah gives two powerful illustrations of the devastation to Edom's wealth that would take place and described it in terms of a mighty and terrible disaster (*v.5*).

Firstly, he gives the picture of thieves breaking into a house. It is inconceivable that robbers entering a dwelling at night would make off with everything that was in the home. They would at least leave something. They may have stolen the most valuable items, but other items would be left. Yet for Edom it would be worse, much worse than that because everything would be taken.

Secondly, the picture moves from criminal activity to the legitimate work of grape pickers in the countryside. Again it is not every grape that is picked. Some would be left because they were missed by accident; others were too small or not ripe enough. The main crop would be gathered in, but not every grape would be picked. Yet for Edom it would be different, very much different, as everything would be taken.

These two pictures are in great contrast with the total devastation to come

The End of a Nation

upon the country of Edom. Its wealth would be completely removed, as would its people. So Edom's wealth could not protect it from the coming judgement. Also other factors in which Edom trusted and took pride could not give the country the needed protection against God's judgement.

Edom's Great Foreign Policy

In *v. 7* we note that Edom felt secure in its alliances with other nations. It was a false security, but Edom felt powerful because it was the chief country in a network of treaties and pacts with other countries. No doubt those pacts were to do with trade, mutual defence and the prosecution of security and peace. Edom would have viewed these other nations as friends and allies and thought they would rally to support Edom in its time of trouble.

The confederate nations are not named but it would undoubtedly include the neighbouring countries of Moab, Ammon and the Arabian tribes. It is possible that there were treaties with the coastal nations of Gaza and Tyre as well as further afield. It all added up to a seemingly secure defensive and protective shield of confederate nations that would support each other in the face of danger and invading foreign armies.

Unfortunately for Edom when the danger came the confederation fell apart under the pressure of self-interest. Edom would send emissaries to the nations of the alliance asking for help. Such envoys though undoubtedly treated with respectful, even lavish hospitality and were escorted back to their own borders, but no help was forthcoming for Edom. Instead of help there would be scheming and devious plots to destroy Edom and all its wealth. The friends of Edom would join the

The Book of Obadiah

invading forces and help set traps to deceive Edom, causing it to be weakened militarily and eventually to be overpowered by the invading army. Even those who had been sustained with all sorts of help from Edom would join in setting traps to deceive Edom. The tragedy for Edom would be that they would not detect these entrapments until it was too late.

Thus Edom's foreign policy like it great wealth would not protect it in the day when the Lord brought His judgement upon the nation.

Edom's Great Wisdom

As *v.8* makes clear Edom was not an educationally backward country. It was an intellectual people, whose understanding and knowledge was held in great reputation. Thus Edom was noted for its wise men. Such men would be advisors and counsellors to the political and military leaders of the nation. It would have been the expectation of the people that with such wisdom they would be able to outsmart and outwit all those who would want to do damage to their country. Yet it was clearly and only the wisdom of men and not the wisdom of God.

Such wisdom is of necessity fallible at best and disastrous at worst. Edom had become corrupt and conceited in its wisdom and despised others as a consequence. The Apostle Paul wrote:

"For it is written, I will destroy the wisdom of the wise, and will bring to nothing the understanding of the prudent. Where is the wise? Where is the scribe? Where is the disputer of this world? Hath not God made foolish the wisdom of this world? For after that in the wisdom of God the world by wisdom knew not God, it pleased God by the foolishness of preaching to save them that believe." (***1 Corinthians 1.19-21***)

The End of a Nation

It is good to be wise and knowledgeable but with the wisdom and knowledge of God that is found in the Bible and is discerned within the human heart by the Spirit of God. The Bible never despises the intellect and academic qualifications are not to be derided. Yet there is a danger, as witnessed in the life and history of Edom. It is possible to be conceited or as the Authorised Version puts it 'puffed up' with pride when academic qualifications are achieved.

Such qualifications give some people a sense of personal power, of elitism, of self-sufficiency and a disdainful view of others who are less qualified. It can lead to a feeling of infallibility, of always thinking that one's views are always right and should be adopted by others. It can lead to hurt pride, anger, bitterness and hurtful words when others do not take on board those views. Thus academic pride can lead to serious repercussions, especially when this is found in church circles. Instead we should remember the words of Oliver Cromwell to the warring theologians of his day, "Remember, brethren, you could be wrong!" We need a constant humbleness to enable us to pursue truth, seek God's help and His wise counsel to us in every situation of life.

In that coming day of judgement, the Lord declared that he would destroy the wise men in Edom and all men of understanding from "the mountains of Esau". (*v.8*) How foolish it is to trust in the wisdom of men and how important it is to seek the wisdom that it from above, namely from the Lord Himself.

So Edom would find that its fortresses, its wealth, its foreign policy of alliances and its wisdom would fail in the coming day of judgement. However, there was one further feature of their national life in which they put great faith.

The Book of Obadiah

Edom's Great Army

Edom had a strong army and prided itself on the strength of its soldiers. The warriors of Edom were powerful, brave and full of determination and are described in *v.9* as "Your warriors, O Teman". Teman was the grandson Esau, the founding father of Edom and his name is used here as an alternative to Edom. However, Teman was also a city in Edom and was the southernmost of the nation's two chief cities and was possibly the capital city. Thus it would be in that city that there would be the concentration of wealth, wisdom, political and military power. Undoubtedly it was here that the army would have been headquartered and from here military decisions would have been taken. It is possible that here the army personnel were trained and that would help to have established the reputation of Edom's warriors.

So Edom would have believed that as a last resort its soldiers would protect the country, even if confederates failed and wealth ran out. The nation took pride in its soldiers, who were physically strong and powerful. They were soldiers with a wonderful reputation.

Today it is possible that with health and a robust physique, to be proud, like Edom. This can especially be true of the young, who have yet to experience the failure of strength and the breakdown of bodily organs. There can be a feeling that the vitality of youth will last forever and a tendency to be impatient with the elderly, the weak, the disabled and the frail. Be sure to take time to learn patience with those who may seem slow, who can't always keep up, who seem to catch on to what you saying very slowly. Remember that the strength and health of youth must give way one day to the weakness and breakdown of health in old age. Don't be like Edom who prided itself in its strength, the mighty power of its armed forces.

The End of a Nation

Obadiah rips away the confidence that the Edomites had in their army, by describing the reaction of those same soldiers in the coming day of judgement. They would be "terrified". A deep fear would descend upon the ranks of armed personnel and no soldier can fight effectively if he is paralysed by fear. Fear is one of the greatest enemies we all face, but Edom's soldiers would be beyond fear and into the realm of terror.

Terror would cause them to defend themselves and their country ineffectively. It would cause them to retreat prematurely and in terrible disarray. It would cause them to disobey orders and fail to see any weaknesses in the enemy ranks, which they might exploit for victory. It would cause them to feel that the whole exercise was a total and complete waste of time and so they would be utterly demoralised. In truth it would be a waste of time, because they were ultimately fighting against Almighty God and no one is able to stand before the Lord.

The result of such poor defensive strategies from the armies would be complete disaster for Edom. Everyone would be in danger and they would be utterly destroyed as a nation. This would be no partial invasion, no peace pacts would be made and no honourable surrender would be available. Once and for all the mountain retreats of Edom would be destroyed and the land laid waste forever.

God never makes false predictions. Everything He says will come to pass. When Obadiah pronounced his prophecy Edom was at the height of its power. Everything seemed to be going wonderfully well. It had strong, high fortresses, great wealth, and strong treaties with other nations, wisdom and wise men in abundance and also a strong, well-trained army. Obadiah's words must have appeared as absurd and yet they came to fulfilment and we have said already, Edom is no more. It has been destroyed and its cliff fortresses are now only a tourist attraction. God's word is true and He always fulfils his promises.

The Book of Obadiah

Reading: Obadiah 3a

"The pride of your heart has deceived you."

As we have seen the prophecy of Obadiah was aimed at the nation of Edom and it was essentially a message of condemnation and prediction of coming doom. One of the main reasons for such judgement was the sin of pride that filled the hearts of the people of Edom.

In our short reading we notice that pride has the ability to deceive, and as we have already noted in our studies in Obadiah it can rob us of our trust in God and of our care for other people. Pride is something that needs to be crushed and driven out of our lives as Christian people. Pride can cause many, many problems and because it is so deceitful we may be under its influence and be unaware and not really notice. We need to take a closer look at this dreadful evil that brings such condemnation from the Lord to the extent that He says, "Pride and arrogancy…do I hate". *(Proverbs 8.13)*

In his book, "The Seven Deadly Sins" Billy Graham lists pride as the first and says, "The first of the seven deadly sins is pride…Pride is thus the mental and moral condition that precedes almost all other sins." While J.C. Ryle wrote, "No sin is so deeply rooted in our nature as pride. It cleaves to us like our skin." And Thomas Hooker wrote of pride, as "the very last and hardest to put off." Pride is a major problem and is not easy to deal with, yet to be effective as Christians and to grow strong in our faith we must deal with it.

To begin with we need to get to an understanding of this problem of pride and then seek ways with the Lord's help to conquer it.

Pride must not be equated with genuine self-respect and the assurance

The End of a Nation

that goes with being aware of personal skills and abilities. Neither is it the same as a true sense of personal dignity or the pleasure that is derived from a job well done or satisfaction in completing something successfully. Pride according to the Oxford Dictionary is "an overweening opinion of one's qualities or merits, arrogant bearing or conduct", while the Collins Dictionary defines pride as "excessive self-esteem, conceit". Thus pride is an inflated ego, an inflated view of one's importance and ability. It is an attitude that breeds insensitivity, intolerance, an unmerited sense of superiority and a despising of others. It should never be encountered amongst true Christian people, but unfortunately we can all be prone to such an attitude.

Pride can prove utterly divisive and that is seen in the New Testament, when the Apostle John wrote about a man named Diotrephes. He loved to have the pre-eminent position in the church and considered himself first. Anyone opposing him was put out of the church fellowship and he reacted strongly against any authority, including that of the apostles. John indicated in his third epistle that such arrogance would not go unpunished and that is confirmed by the writer of the Proverbs: "The Lord detests all the proud of heart. Be sure of this: They will not go unpunished." (16.5) We need to remember that God hates pride and he wants to kill it within our hearts and minds. Every genuine Christian hates and loathes what God hates and loathes and thus we must wage a genuine war on the forces and strongholds of pride that may possess our minds. Are we proud? How do we know?

Pride is detected in a number of ways. Firstly, personal pride causes our thoughts to dwell upon self and our own needs to the exclusion of concern for the needs of others. Secondly, pride looks for the praise of people and demands respect from others. That was exactly the position of the religious leaders in the day of Jesus; they took pride in their status. Thirdly, pride is rarely satisfied, as Thomas Brooks wrote, "A

The Book of Obadiah

proud soul is content with nothing". Fourthly, pride cannot accept and reacts violently against correction or rebuke, as George Duncan wrote, "There is nothing that human pride resents so much as to be rebuked". Fifthly, pride is intolerant of the ability and success of others and is wounded by it. As someone has written, "When a proud man hears another praised, he thinks himself injured". We see a clear example of that in the Old Testament when the wonderful success of David provoked King Saul to jealous, unreasoning and vengeful anger. Saul's pride made him too big for his boots and he was eventually rejected as king of Israel and we read these words, "And Samuel said (to Saul), When you were little in your own sight, you were made the head of the tribes of Israel, and the Lord anointed you king of Israel…because you have rejected the word of the Lord, he has rejected you from being king." *(1 Samuel 15.17/23)*

Pride can become the basis of so much evil. It can make people ungrateful and unappreciative. The proud man seldom says "thank you" because he never thinks that he gets as much as he deserves. Pride as we have seen can lead to the sins of jealousy, of anger, of revenge, of gossip, of rudeness, of deceitfulness and of indifference to the needs of others. Thus if we deal with our pride, many other sins will be dealt with at the same time.

The worst aspect of pride is that it can close our minds to our deepest need, which is the spiritual need of the soul. Unless we are aware of that deep inner need then we will never cry out to God for His salvation. The first step in becoming a true Christian and experiencing the reality of the Lord in our lives is to recognise our need. The need for our sins to be forgiven, for the barrier between God and us to be removed, for the God-shaped emptiness within us to be filled and for us to have contact with the living God. Pride may stop us admitting such needs and will prevent us looking to the Lord Jesus who is the

The End of a Nation

only one who can meet those deepest of all needs. The pride of the human heart will keep many people out of Heaven, as Alan Redpath wrote, "Pride is the idolatrous worship of ourselves, and that is the national religion of hell." The worst form of pride therefore says, 'I don't need God and can manage successfully without Him.' What disillusionment will eventually come upon such proud people?

How do we deal with pride within our own hearts? Are there any principles, which enable pride to be undercut in our lives and to be controlled and hindered from taking root and producing its awful fruit? Let me outline six principles that may help us in this whole area of dealing with selfish pride.

1. *The need to see the greatness of Almighty God.*

As we read God's Word each day we come face to face with the reality of God. We find that He is a great God. His characteristics are way beyond anything we possess and before such a God we are so insignificant and small. God is eternal, with no beginning and end. We in comparison are temporal with beginning and an end here on planet earth. God is the creator of heaven and earth and as we consider the vastness of the universe how small we are before such a God. In contrast we are unable to create anything, because creation is to make something out of nothing. We are certainly incapable of such an exercise.

God is omniscient. He knows everything and no new knowledge can be given to Him. In contrast we are extremely limited in what we know and understand and that problem is compounded, because the disciplines of learning become more and more specialist and narrowly defined.

God is omnipotent. He is all-powerful, as he sustains the great creation and rules in the affairs of men. He builds up kingdoms and empires

The Book of Obadiah

and then tears them down and sets the boundaries in the affairs of men. As individuals we have no such power and even those in the political arena have little or no influence to affect policies, as our elected officials seem incapable of altering the course of history.

God is omnipresent. He is everywhere at once, because God is spirit. *(John 4.24)* That is why we can have fellowship with Him and enjoy His presence wherever we are and however many we may be. What a contrast to the limitations we experience within the confines of our human body.

God is holy. There is nothing impure within the character of God and nothing of immorality. The difference could not be starker as we consider our own sinfulness and inability to control the sinful urges we experience.

God is immutable. He is utterly unchanging in his character, aims and motives and in contrast we are so changeable as human beings. We have major mood swings and are so often governed by our feelings and lack a consistency in our reactions to people and circumstances.

God is love. He is the God of deepest compassion. His love never changes and is immeasurable and limitless. He loves the worst of sinners, the blasphemer, the atheist, the most evil of people, even though he hates their sin. We fail to love like that and so often our love can turn to indifference and even hatred. We are thankful for God's love that caused Jesus to die for our sins.

So the more we view the great God of the Bible the more we stand in awe of his person. This puts who we are into perspective and helps to deal with pride as we recognise our utter insignificance before such a great God. We are mere specks of dust in the presence of such greatness and yet we are the recipients of His wonderful compassion and in consequence we turn to Him with thankful hearts.

The End of a Nation

2. *The need to keep focused upon the Lord Jesus*

As we view the Son of God as revealed in Holy Scripture we become aware of the fact that we are utterly indebted to Him for our salvation. As it dawns upon our mind that we could not save ourselves and could contribute nothing towards the gift of eternal life we become aware of how significant He is and how insignificant we are. As people who broke the law of God and who could produce nothing of eternal merit we needed someone to meet our needs. That someone was the Lord Jesus Christ.

The essential truth is that we needed to pay a debt to God for breaking His laws. However, we were utterly incapable of even making a contribution to that debt. The result was that we were condemned to the punishment that the Law demanded. Yet Christ in deep love entered the human race and sacrificed Himself on the cross for our sins. What we were incapable of doing He was more than capable of achieving and it humbles us to think that without Him we could never be saved. What man could not do, Christ did and we thank God for that. The hymn writer put it this way,

> "There was no other good enough to pay the price for sin,
> He only could unlock the gate of Heaven and let us in."

3. *The need to look at the Holy Spirit*

Pride is dealt a severe blow when we realise that we could never be saved without the work of the Holy Spirit. It was the Holy Spirit who drew our attention to our spiritual need and made us realise that we were sinners in need of forgiveness. It was He who brought a deep conviction upon our minds and hearts. Without that convicting and burdening work of the Holy Spirit we could never have been saved.

The Book of Obadiah

Also we would never have understood the significance of Christ and His work on the cross without the Holy Spirit giving us that insight. He opened our eyes to see our need of the Saviour and gave us the desire and the will to repent and believe the Gospel. So we take no pride in being saved as a reward for effort because it was all the converting work of the Holy Spirit.

4. The need to obey God's Word

Each day the Christian should be spending time reading and meditating upon the precious Word of God, the Holy Bible. This is not simply to build up head knowledge and collect facts that are contained in the Bible, but is the result of a deep desire to know God and to understand how He wants us to live each day. In the Bible we find the defining principles for Christian living and yet to obey them can mean sacrifice, hardship and opposition. Yet when the Christian believer is determined to live for God, no matter what the cost, then there is no room for pride or overt egotistical behaviour.

The Bible also enables us to see how servants of God from the past conducted their lives. It shows how they conquered pride and other sins and that is an incentive for us to imitate their successes. We are also told about their failures and the pitfalls they fell into and they stand out as warnings for us to avoid similar defeats in our own lives. We also come face to face with the Lord Jesus, particularly in the Gospels and his life is the greatest example of a surrendered life. His was a life lived under authority, the authority of His Father's will and that involved giving up the privileges and surrounding glory of deity for the poverty and limitation of life in a human body. Though he was always deity, He volunteered to give up His privileges in order to die to be our Saviour. Such willing humility should encourage us also to surrender pride that we too may be able to fully serve the Lord.

The End of a Nation

5. *The need to pray each day*

Every day we need to draw close to the Lord in prayer. The closer we come into contact with the Saviour the more like Him we become. He served others in love and humbleness and so should we. As we pray we ask the Lord for a right attitude of self-sacrifice and a willingness to see the needs of others and help alleviate them. As we bow before the Lord in prayer we learn to fight pride and all that hinders the free flowing work of God in our lives.

6. *The need to do all we can to help others*

We must seek the Saviour's help to see as He sees. He recognised needs and so should we. There are hurting people in our communities and so often we don't see the hurt and so do nothing to help. We need a deep sensitivity to people and a willingness to help meet the needs of others whenever we come across them. Yet at the same time we must not lose sight of the fact that people's greatest need is to hear the Gospel, so that they can believe in the Lord Jesus and be saved with the wonderful gift of forgiveness and eternal life. It is not always easy to present the Gospel, especially with people who are hostile or indifferent, but that should never cause us to lose sight of this vital work of leading men and women to Christ. Pride will always hinder the true work of evangelism.

So the battle with pride can be waged and as we view the greatness of God, the work of Christ on the Cross, the work of the Holy Spirit in our hearts, the reality of His precious word, the vitality of prayer and the needs of other people we are humbled and bow before the Lord in reverence and worship. So lets avoid the deceitfulness of pride and serve the Lord in true faithfulness.

The Book of Obadiah

Reading: Obadiah 10-14

"For your violence against your brother Jacob, shame shall cover you. And you shall be cut off forever. In the day that you stood on the other side – in the day that strangers carried captive his forces, when foreigners entered his gates and cast lots for Jerusalem – even you were as one of them. But you should not have gazed on the day of your brother. In the day of his captivity; nor should you have rejoiced over the children of Judah in the day of their destruction; nor should you have spoken proudly in the day of distress. You should not have entered the gate of my people in the day of their calamity. Indeed, you should not have gazed on their afflictions in the day of their calamity. Nor laid hands on their substance in the day of their calamity. You should not have stood at the crossroads to cut off those among them who escaped: nor should you have delivered up those among them who remained in the day of distress."

The prophecy of Obadiah is aimed at the nation of Edom and is a pronouncement of their future destruction. They had proved to be an arrogant and proud nation, but our reading also indicates that they were a violent and destructive people.

It is expressly stated that Edom would be 'cut off' because of its violent behaviour directed towards its 'brother Jacob'. (*v.10*) So Edom's violence had been focused specifically upon the nation of Israel. The two countries had a common border but also had a common ancestry as they had descended from the same family. Both nations could trace their genealogy back to Isaac and Abraham. Edom's ancestry went through Isaac's son Esau, while Israel's was through

The End of a Nation

Isaac's son Jacob and that is why Obadiah used the name 'Jacob' as opposed to Israel or Judah to describe the chosen people of God. He was simply emphasising the close family connection between the two nations. Indeed the brothers Esau and Jacob had been twins and so their family connection could not have been closer. And to make the point abundantly clear, so clear that no one could miss it he used the phrase 'your brother Jacob'.

Edom's violent behaviour towards Israel would bring about two consequences. Firstly, as a nation they would be 'covered with shame'. This seems to indicate the first phase in Edom's punishment as a nation. They would be overrun and taken captive as a people. They would experience the shame of being ruled by others, of being deported and taken into captivity. That would be a calamity for such a proud people and the humiliation would make them feel utterly degraded.

Secondly, the time would come when they would lose their national identity. The nation of Edom would become extinct or as Obadiah wrote, 'you shall be cut off (or destroyed) forever'. Thus the shame was merely a prelude to a more compounded judgement upon the nation of Edom. History tells us in the words of Charles Feinberg, that Edom "was ultimately reduced by John Hyrcanus of the Maccabean dynasty and lost their national existence under the Romans." They had as a nation chosen to raise their hand in violent opposition towards God's chosen people Israel and they could not do that with impunity. They faced the consequences of their own actions.

The context of Edom's reactions towards Israel was that an invading army had swept into Judah. It was the armies of the Chaldees and Edom had chosen to give Israel no support and had instead assumed an attitude of overt hostility towards God's people. They had proffered no help to Israel in her time of trouble. That is a challenge to us as

The Book of Obadiah

Christians that in our own lives, it is vital that we offer the best help and show real compassion to anyone who is experiencing trouble and difficulty. This is true even if we feel that the troubles were in some way self-inflicted. We must not pass by with indifference and ignore the needs of others. We must show compassion and not hostility towards such people.

Edom's reactions towards Israel in its time of trouble are outlined by Obadiah.

1. Edom had stood aloof (*v.11*)

It was a sad day when foreign armies swept into the great capital city of Jerusalem. The wealth of that city was stolen and carried away, and the invaders had gambled or 'cast lots' to determine who would take the plunder of that city. The invading army was a coalition and each would take something and where they couldn't agree then lots were cast for the privilege of extra plunder from the city.

Edom's reaction had been wilful indifference. They had stood aloof from Israel's troubles and that literally means that they 'stood on the other side'. We are reminded of the parable Jesus told of a man journeying from Jerusalem to Jericho who was robbed and beaten and left for dead on the side of the road. A priest came along and 'passed by on the other side'. He remained aloof and refused to help the injured man. Later a Levite came by and looked at the man but 'passed by on the other side'. He too refused to help and remained indifferent to the man who was dying. Both the priest and Levite really identified with the attackers rather than with the attacked. We thank God for the Good Samaritan who went and helped the man and saved his life. Jesus says to us as we see that act of goodness to go and do likewise.

The End of a Nation

Yet Edom's indifference to Israel's plight did not leave them guiltless. They were not in some neutral condition. Their reactions were essentially passive involvement, they had in essence joined the enemies of Israel, as Obadiah wrote, "you were like one of them". Edom was like one of the enemies of Israel. Hailey writes, "When Edom should have felt sympathy for the humiliated and suffering kinsman, the Lord charges, "even thou was as one of them," the enemies."

Thus there is no neutral position as we view those in need. We either do something to help or compound their problems by indifference and aloofness.

2. Edom had gloated *(v.12)*

Edom's passive indifference at Israel being invaded turned to a sort of a derisive jeering at Jerusalem's plight. Again Obadiah used the phrase, "your brother" and says you should not have gloated or 'looked down on your brother'. They showed no pity for Jerusalem's plight and felt no sadness at Israel's distress. Instead they insolently gloated and rejoiced at Israel's troubles. They delighted and expressed that delight with glee that Jerusalem was in such desperate trouble and suffering so much. At that moment in history Edom seemed to be free from trouble and so gloated arrogantly and looked down upon poor defeated Israel.

We must never for one moment join in any form of mocking or gloating at the misfortunes of others. We must never think that because we are fairly free of troubles that we have God's particular blessing or because we may be inundated with troubles that somehow we have lost God's particular blessing. We remember that there were people gathered around the cross of Christ to gloat, to jeer and to rejoice in his suffering, pain and death. They failed to realise that in love He was dying for the sins of the world.

The Book of Obadiah

We must be careful that when we view the troubles of others that we don't give the impression of gloating and saying things like, 'they deserved it' or 'we are glad that they failed'. No we should obey with sincerity the injunction of Scripture that says, "Rejoice with them that do rejoice and weep with them that weep". (***Romans 12.15***)

3. Edom had boasted *(v.12)*

In the day of Israel's trouble and distress when their capital city of Jerusalem was invaded and ransacked Edom had been boastful. They had 'spoken proudly' or as Feinberg writes, "they used arrogant language in exultation over their conquered enemy." They looked down and rejoiced over Jerusalem's trouble but proudly boasted of their own impregnable and unassailable fortresses. They believed that their defences could never be breached and boastfully announced that to Israel.

There is no room for boasting and pride in the make up of the Christian. Our only boast is in the work of Christ on the cross. His death means life to those who believe on Him. As a hymn writer put it, "In the cross of Christ I glory". We have nothing else to glory in, save Christ and Him crucified.

4. Edom had marched into Jerusalem *(v.13)*

Edom moved from simply looking and gloating to involvement and action in the deeper destruction of Israel. Edom's attitude and words had been bad enough, but a further step was taken in the downward path of sinfulness when they actually joined the invading armies and entered Jerusalem. This was opportunistic as they seized their chance to gain from the misfortune of their brother nation. Here was their chance to gain something for nothing and to exploit the weakness of

The End of a Nation

the people of God. So Edom marched through the gates of the cities of Israel and compounded the troubles of Jacob.

Hailey writes, "It is a travesty today on our society and its integrity that when disaster strikes a city or countryside the National Guard must be called out to protect the goods – not from the unfortunate people's enemies, but from the plundering hands of their own neighbours. Times change little, and humanity not at all."

5. Edom stole from Israel *(v.13)*

Edom had looked down upon Jehovah's weakened and plundered people with covetous eyes. They wanted a share in the wealth of Israel, which was being seized and distributed amongst the invading armies. Israel's trouble was emphasised with a double statement. Firstly, it is described as a 'calamity' and secondly as 'the day of their disaster'. These are strong statements and indicate how serious and terrible the events were for the nation of Israel.

Yet Edom with selfish covetousness joined in the general looting of Israel. They too plundered the wealth of Jerusalem. They did not hesitate to exploit the weakness of their brother nation. Edom compounded its sin and would face the judgement of God.

6. Edom killed fugitives *(v.14)*

Edom went even further in its vindictive approach to dominating Israel. They posted sentries at the various crossroads leading out and away from Jerusalem and there they intercepted Israelite fugitives who were trying to escape from the destruction of the invading armies. Maybe some of those escaping people were desperately trying to reach the River Jordan and hide in the undergrowth or to cross the river and find refuge in the semi-desert conditions on the eastern side. Others

The Book of Obadiah

may have tried to escape to the arid regions of the south, while others might have been fleeing to the hills and mountain regions. Yet for most of them their efforts were in vain and ended in tragedy. The Edomites cut off their retreat and murdered them and presumably robbed them of any valuables the retained. It was cruel exploitation of a traumatised people.

7. Edom sold fugitives *(v.14)*

Some of those fleeing Israelites were not put to death by the Edomites but were captured and handed over to the invading armies. Presumably these would have been the more important persons such as officials from the Israelite army or government. No doubt Edom would have gained from such actions and would have received payment. Those prisoners would have become slaves and been deported from their native land.

So we see that in these seven ways Edom had exploited the weakness of Israel and compounded her troubles and tribulations. Edom's attitude was indifference, her words were gloating and boastful, while her actions were to exploit, with very great cruelty. Israel had enough troubles without the added afflictions imposed by the nation of Edom.

How important it is that we show compassion and help alleviate the burdens of others, especially those that are hurting, discouraged and feeling down. I remember the elderly lady who lived in our street when we lived in the English Midlands. She was blind in one eye and was confined to a wheel chair because both legs had been amputated. She lived alone and could only live on the ground floor of her house. Clearly she was lonely and at times very sad and we did what we could to visit, to remember her at Christmas and birthdays and to try and encourage her. On sunny days she opened her front door and sat there in her wheel chair just a metre or so from the front gate and the

The End of a Nation

pavement. She told me with a choking voice that people walked that pavement and never looked at her and certainly didn't say anything. She was ignored and felt deeply hurt. She wasn't seeking a conversation, just an acknowledgement with 'Hello'. To take a little interest and bring a little joy to her life didn't cost much and didn't take long, but the attitude of indifference and actions of aloofness deepened her sense of rejection and loss. How careful we should be that we bring encouragement and not discouragement to people we meet.

I remember hearing of the minister who was telephoned in the middle of the night to say that one of his congregation was drunk. The man had a problem with drink and was trying to fight the power of alcohol. The minister immediately got into his car to pick the man up and bring him home, while his wife started to make up a bed in the spare room. The minister's son enquired why this was being done. The man was drunk and would be sick and surely it was all a waste of time. His mother said, 'Tonight he is drunk, but tomorrow he will be sober and will be so ashamed and will need all the love and support we can give him.' She like her husband realised that the drunken man was down but they would not compound his problems but do everything to help him get up and get on to live the Christian life.

We all have frailties and weaknesses and it is so easy to take our eyes off our own needs and concentrate with a critical eye upon the failings of others. In a subtle way by condemning them we justify ourselves and try to give the impression that all is well with us. Let's see beyond the failings in other people and see their potential in Christ and try with God's grace to bring them to that place where they can fully serve the Lord. Let's build up and be constructive, rather than tear down and be destructive. Let us take warning from Obadiah's message to Edom that God punishes those who inflict evil upon others, especially upon those who are already troubled and hurting.

The Book of Obadiah

Reading: Obadiah 15-16

"For the day of the LORD upon all the nations is near; as you have done it shall be done to you; your reprisal shall return upon your own head. For as you drank on my holy mountain, so shall all the nations drink continually; yes, they shall drink, and swallow, and they shall be as though they had never been."

The message of Obadiah is aimed at the nation of Edom and is a foretelling of future punishment for the Edomites. This was due to their inward attitude of pride and arrogance, especially towards the people of Israel and also their outward actions of cruelty and vindictive violence towards the nation of Israel.

In our reading we are introduced to one of the great themes of the Bible, namely, "The day of the Lord". This is a term that occurs many times in the Holy Scriptures and is sometimes referred to as "that day" or "the great day". It is used so frequently that it must be considered as a highly significant concept. The idea is not that this is a literal, twenty-four hour day but is essentially a time of judgement from God upon those who are His enemies. It is a time of terror and overthrow for those who are opposed to the Lord and a time of deliverance and redemption for those who trust Him.

Ultimately 'the day of the Lord' ushers in the final judgement upon mankind and will culminate in the new heavens and a new earth. So what Obadiah has done is to broaden the scope of his prophetic statements from the local and imminent judgement upon the nation of Edom and look down the ages of time to the consummation of the ages at the Second Coming of Christ. Also he widens the scope of God's judgement from simply one nation to embrace and encompass all peoples. So the first part of v. 15 indicates two aspects of the Day of the Lord.

The End of a Nation

1. **It is Near**. The Bible gives us a great deal of information about this great day and a number of its characteristics are outlined for us but its exact time is never emphasised. Yet the prophet says 'It is near'! However, Obadiah wrote nearly 3,000 years ago and it seems absurd for him to say that it is near. Four things need to be said about this. Firstly, the idea of nearness was literally true of Edom. They as it were faced their own 'day of the Lord' and their doom was waiting at the door. Secondly, in a similar way other nations have found their 'day of the Lord' was imminent and the judgement of the Lord fell upon them. This has been witnessed in Biblical times with nations such as Egypt, Babylon, Assyria and even Israel and Judah. Thirdly, imminence needs to be seen from the Lord's perspective rather than ours and He dwells not in time but in eternity, and what seems long and significant to us, is transcended as nothing by Almighty God. Fourthly, everyone should live as if the 'day of the Lord' could occur at any moment. We should, as Christians, live in eager expectation of the Saviour's imminent return.

It is said that when the saintly Robert Murray McCheyne once asked his students if they thought that the Lord would return that night. They thought about it and replied in the negative. No they did not think the Saviour's return would be that night. Of course, they turned out to be right. However, with great solemnity McCheyne replied, "Therefore be ye ready: for in such an hour as you think not the Son of Man cometh". (*Matthew 24.44*)

2. **It is for All Nations**. Again Obadiah expands the thought of the 'day of the Lord' from the localised situation specifically dealing with the one nation of Edom and makes it universal in application to encompass the nations of the world. Some of those nations are mentioned towards the end of this great prophecy. Biblically the nations who are specified as facing God's judgement are those who

The Book of Obadiah

have dealings with Israel and they are judged for how they have reacted to and treated God's earthly chosen people. One commentator summarised it as follows:

"Remote as was Obadiah's situation from this still future period of judgement, he yet saw, with the peculiar telescopic vision so characteristic of inspired prophecy, that the principle of retribution whereby the Edomites would pay for their iniquity is not confined to this one people." (Frank E. Gaebelein)

The heart of *v.15* gives us the essential principle of God's judgement. This is the key to the book of Obadiah and explains why Edom eventually perished as a nation. The principle is clearly enunciated:

"As you have done, it will be done to you".

Another way of stating this principle is in the words of the Apostle Paul:

"Be not deceived; God is not mocked: for whatsoever a man soweth, that shall he also reap." (***Galatians 6.7***)

So it is the principle that what we sow, we reap. In the manner in which we have treated others, so we will also be treated. As we have done to others, so it shall be done unto us. We need to be very careful in all our dealings with others. There are many facets in modern society that are taken for granted but cause enormous damage to the feelings and emotions of individuals. Anger, rudeness, aggressive behaviour, indifference, gossip and deceitful behaviour are so often commonplace in many circles. Many of us may have been victims of such behaviour and still feel deeply the hurt of it all to this day. How important it is that we remember how wounded we felt in our spirit when it happened to us and make sure that we never inflict such wounds on others, no

The End of a Nation

matter what people have said or done to us. We are called by God to act in the way described by the Apostle Paul:

"Let all bitterness, and wrath, and anger, and clamour, and evil speaking, be put away from you, with all malice: And by kind one to another, tenderhearted, forgiving one another, even as God for Christ's sake has forgiven you." (*Ephesians 4.31-32*)

It is not easy to obey the injunctions of those words but we have the resources of God to help us. Those resources are threefold. Firstly, there is the facility of prayer. If we fail to pray we can never live in the way God intended for His people. Secondly, we have His Word that cleanses us and also focuses our attention upon our greatest example of such living, namely the Saviour Himself. The more we see Him, the more like Him we can become. Thirdly, we have, as Christians, the indwelling Spirit of God. Certainly without His work in us we could never begin to live in the way the Lord expects. So with the aid of genuine prayer, regular and in-depth reading of the Bible and the inward activity of the Holy Spirit we can begin to live as the Lord wants us to.

However, Edom had failed in this respect and their doom was sealed. As they had done, it would be done unto them. Their deeds would return upon their own head. We can imagine that when this judgement fell upon Edom and unpleasant things happened to them they would be haunted by the fact that they had done similar things to others in the past. The invading forces that would exploit Edom were doing exactly what Edom had done with Israel. It was just retribution and they had no one to blame but themselves. It would be seen as self-evident that God's judgement was just, fair and equitable. Their punishment was a true reflection of their crimes.

The Book of Obadiah

The principle of judgement is illustrated in *v.16*, where Edom is pictured as desecrating God's holy mountain. Indeed the Lord refers to it as "my holy mountain". This has to be the mountain of Jerusalem on which God's temple, the place where Israel worshipped, was located. It was in that city that God had chosen to place His Name, as is clearly indicated in *2 Chronicles 6.6:*

"But I have chosen Jerusalem, that my name might be there; and have chosen David to be over my people Israel."

So the mountain was holy because that was the city of God. It was also holy because it was specifically set apart as the place for Israel to worship God. In no other city in the kingdom were people allowed to build temples or raise altars. True worship to God could only be conducted as a collective activity for the nation in the place where God had placed his name. There, in the temple, the High Priest, together with the priests and levites were kept busy fulfilling the Old Testament requirements concerning sacrifices and offerings to the Lord. There too they taught the people the Word of God and instructed them in the commandments and laws of God, as given to Moses.

So as the Lord possessed that mountain and claimed it as His by saying, "my holy mountain", any violation was a direct and open insult to the Lord. Edom had therefore insulted the Lord by drinking on that consecrated place. The idea seems to be that Edom partied in Jerusalem and drank to excess. Like any drunk they went beyond the accepted limits of normal and controlled behaviour and did things that were outside the norms of accepted behaviour. Consumption of alcohol does need to be carefully controlled and the Bible condemns drunkenness and excess. There is victory even over this evil through Jesus Christ and many an alcoholic has been grateful to God for deliverance from drink's power and the change of life for the better, which the Lord has given.

The End of a Nation

The Edomites were pictured as indulging in a drunken orgy upon the holy mountain of God. This undoubtedly included serious drinking by the victorious invading army, but also would be a picture of the excessive violence and cruelty they exercised towards God's people. They were like a violently out of control drunk who stops at nothing to inflict pain and humiliation on others. Yet it was not just Edom who had behaved in this way as the description applies to "all nations". This may be simply a reference to the coalition of invading forces under the leadership of the Chaldees, whom Edom joined. It may, however, have much wider significance concerning the nations who through the ages have indulged in oppressive behaviour towards God's people. Many nations, like Edom, have exploited Israel when she was weak and they would all face the severe judgement of the Lord.

Their punishment would be to 'drink and drink' and not to stop. They would 'drink continually'. This may not seem on the surface to be a significant punishment until we realise what they are drinking. The idea is that as these nations had drunk the cup of hatred and aggression, so they would drink the cup of God's wrath to their own destruction.

This picture is detailed for us in the book of Jeremiah. He talked of the "the wine cup of fury", and in *Jeremiah 25.15-17,* he wrote:

"For thus saith the Lord God of Israel unto me; Take the wine cup of this fury at my hand, and cause all the nations, to whom I send thee to drink it. And they shall drink, and be moved, and be mad, because of the sword that I will send among them. Then took I the cup at the Lord's hand, and made all the nations to drink, unto whom the Lord had sent me."

Later in the same chapter Jeremiah gives a list of those nations who would drink from this cup of fury. One of those nations was the people

The Book of Obadiah

of Edom. Jeremiah went on to point out that the nations will have no choice, but will have to partake of this cup of fury, for he further wrote:

"Therefore thou shalt say unto them, Thus saith the Lord of hosts, the God of Israel; Drink ye, and be drunken, and spue, and fall, and rise no more, because of the sword which I will send among you. And it shall be, if they refuse to take the cup at thine hand to drink, then shalt thou say unto them, Thus saith the Lord of hosts, Ye shall certainly drink." (***Jeremiah 25.27-28***)

So Jeremiah like Obadiah saw in prophetic vision the nations being compelled to drink this cup of fury. They would have no choice because this was God's judgement upon them. The cup seems to be the arising of the war-lust of nations. There have always been wars and battles, but this appears to be a blind, irrational desire for cruelty and vengeance for no apparent reason and for no national gain. We have seen nations slip into those kinds of warfare situations throughout history and not least in the twentieth and twenty-first centuries. Indeed Gaebelein comments on these verses by writing: "Who will doubt that we are living in a day when this age-old lust has been revived and the world has been drinking the cup of fury as never before?"

The result of drinking from that cup of fury according to Jeremiah is that such nations will "rise no more", while Obadiah wrote, "and they shall be as though they had not been". Such, nations, including Edom will cease to exist and there will be little or no evidence that they ever existed and certainly there would be nothing to indicate that they were once very strong, powerful and rich nations. Today we have no real indication from the ancient ruins just how great and strong Edom was in its heyday. Those silent cities of the forgotten past only echo to the voices of curious tourists, while the once vibrant interaction of trade and commerce have long since gone.

The End of a Nation

Thus we see the effects of 'the day of the Lord'. The nations who are dealt with during that time of judgement have swallowed down the cup of divine wrath or fury and have been utterly wiped out.

Obadiah's direct reference to 'the day of the Lord' is very brief and accords fully with the brevity of the whole of the book. However, we would miss the undoubted application to the present world if we fail to see the warning for any nation that persists in evil aggression and wilfully ignores God's laws.

There is personal application and that is that we cannot persist in flouting the laws of God with impunity. Sooner or later there will be retribution and we will face the awful judgement of God's wrath. It is so important that we heed the message of the Gospel and find refuge and safety in Jesus Christ, by receiving Him into our hearts by faith as our Lord and Saviour.

The Book of Obadiah

Reading: Obadiah 17-18

"But on Mount Zion there shall be deliverance, and there shall be holiness; the house of Jacob shall possess their possessions. The house of Jacob shall be a fire, and the house of Joseph a flame; but the house of Esau shall be stubble; they shall kindle them and devour them, and no survivor shall remain of the house of Esau. For the Lord has spoken."

Obadiah's prophecy is directed towards one of Israel's enemies, the country of Edom. It is prediction of total destruction for the nation because of their pride and violence towards Israel. The warning has wider application to all nations who violate the integrity of the nation of Israel.

In these verses we see attention move to Israel and the first word of v.17 indicates that there is a contrast between what has gone before and what comes afterwards. That word is 'but'. In the previous verses we witnessed the outpouring of judgement upon the nations during 'the day of the Lord'. There seemed no place to hide and no place of safety, yet there was one safe place. That place was mount Zion. This was the highest part of Jerusalem and the ultimate goal of pilgrimage. In that place and that place alone there will be 'deliverance'. At that time Israel would enjoy safety, namely deliverance from her enemies.

Such deliverance will be available because the Lord will be there with His heavenly army as they destroy the Gentile nations opposed to God. Yet at the same time there will be holiness on Mount Zion. Those on Mount Zion will be both saved and sanctified and it is not possible to have one without the other. To be sanctified means to be made holy. That is to take on the character of Christ. It carries the idea of being set apart for the unique purposes of serving God and bringing glory to His name. So at that time Israel would enjoy holiness, namely deliverance from defilement.

The End of a Nation

At a personal level we can say that a Christian is both saved and sanctified. There was that glorious day when we received Christ into our lives. We believed that when He died on the cross He died for our sins. We recognised our need to be forgiven and cleansed from our sin if we were ever to know God and one day enter His presence in Heaven. At the point of faith in Jesus Christ, God performed a miracle in us and forgave our sin and made us good enough for Heaven. We were then called to demonstrate that faith by a life of sanctified, holy living. Sanctification of the Christian is seen both as a position and a process.

1. Position: this is our standing in Christ. When we received Him into our lives He washed all our sins away and God then looked at us and saw us in Christ. We are clothed with His righteousness and our spiritual condition is one of holiness. That is why a songwriter could pen the words, "I am covered over with the robe of righteousness that Jesus gives to me". In Christ God considers us holy.

2. Process: the position of holiness that we have in Christ must be developed into a daily life of holy living. This is known as the process of sanctification where our lives gradually take on the characteristics of Jesus Christ. So we learn to be governed by His Spirit and learn to react and act in ways that he would and so we learn obedience to the will of God and learn to live in holiness.

The apostle Peter wrote, "So be ye holy in all conversation, because it is written be ye holy for I am holy." (***1 Peter 1.15-16***)

Those delivered and sanctified on Mount Zion would also be enriched, as Obadiah reminded us when he wrote that memorable sentence, "and the house of Jacob shall possess their possessions". No doubt the use of the name 'Jacob' to describe Israel served to remind Edom again that their two nations were closely related. Yet at the time of Obadiah Israel

The Book of Obadiah

was in dire circumstances. Invading forces had overrun them and they had been stripped of control of their land and cities. They had been dispossessed and had lost their land, possessions, wealth, dignity, freedom and independence as they were killed and deported. It was a sad time for Israel and Edom triumphed and gloried in their strength in contrast with its brother nation.

However, the day would come when the roles would be reversed. Edom would then be in trouble from invading armies. Edom would be desolate and denied nationhood and its people would be impoverished and destitute. The House of Jacob would be strong in that coming day and would 'possess its possessions'. What a glorious day that will be for Israel. Their possessions consisted of the land of Canaan that had been given in promise to Abraham, Isaac and Jacob. It stretched from the River Euphrates to the river of Egypt. Israel had only ever enjoyed that expanse of land under its control during the reigns of David and Solomon. In that coming day Israel would again be reinstated in the territories, which God had given them of old, and then Israel would be enriched, namely delivered from dispossession and poverty.

There is an application to you and me as Christians for we are also called upon to 'possess our possessions'. We have innumerable possessions and wealth in Jesus Christ. Clearly these are not material or financial but are of a far higher value than simply those things that can be handled, seen and heard. God's riches are spiritual and are of infinitely more value than the material. The list of possessions is utterly endless but let us consider just a few:

1. The possession of answered prayer. What a joy when we come into the presence of God with a burden to pray and then to see Him bring about the answer. That strengthens our faith and enriches our soul. It is said that, in nineteenth century Bristol in England, atheism

The End of a Nation

could not raise its head, because of one man. That man was George Mullar who ran an orphanage for dozens of children. He saw them all clothed and fed and never asked people for money. He talked with God and saw God answer his prayers in wonderful and sometimes miraculous ways. As long as that man was alive he was proof, even to sceptics, of the reality of God. Such a life of prayer is available for all God's people. Do we possess our possessions?

2. The possession of knowing God's will. God has a plan and a purpose for our lives as Christians and it is important that we know that plan. When we know God's will and see it worked out in our lives we are enriched and a ministry of grace reaches out to others and we are a blessing both to our fellow Church members and to those outside the fellowship. We understand the guidelines for God's will through His Holy Word, the Bible. That is why we need to read it and meditate upon it each day. Do we possess our possessions?

3. **The possession of the fruit of the Spirit.** In Galatians chapter five the apostle Paul mentions nine manifestations of the fruit of the Spirit. These were wonderfully exemplified in the life of Christ and need to be seen in His followers. Those manifestations are unselfish love, fullness of joy, a deep and abiding peace of heart and life, a patient and gentle demeanour, the qualities of goodness, faithfulness, meekness and self control. To experience the work of the Holy Spirit in our lives truly brings out these wonderful characteristics and enriches our lives as Christian people. Do we possess our possessions?

So with the aid of prayer, God's Word and God's Holy Spirit we can as Christian believers learn to possess our possessions and enter into the most enriching spiritual life it is possible to experience.

The description of Israel's transformed situation from defeated and

The Book of Obadiah

demoralised to victorious and powerful is further developed in *v.18*, with the nation being figuratively portrayed as a fire. It is interesting to notice that Israel is described in two ways:

1. The House of Jacob. We have already encountered the name 'Jacob' to describe Israel in *v.10* and *v.17*. This has been used to describe the close link between the two nations. Jacob and Esau were brothers and descended from their father Isaac and their grandfather Abraham. The brothers were actually twins. From Esau the older brother came the nation of Edom to whom this short prophetic book is addressed and from Jacob came the nation of Israel. However, here in v.18 it might be more a reference to the Southern Kingdom of Judah, which was formed after the partition of Israel and consisted of southern Palestine with the capital city being Jerusalem.

2. The House of Joseph. Joseph's life and character are recorded for us in the first book of the Bible, Genesis. He was one of the twelve sons of Israel and those twelve sons through their descendants became the twelve tribes of Israel. However, there was no tribe named 'Joseph', instead his two sons each gave their names to tribes and each inherited portions of territory in the Promised Land. Joseph's sons were called Ephraim and Manasseh and their tribal areas were located in the Northern Kingdom when Israel divided into two parts. Their combined strength was the dominant power in the Northern Kingdom and so the reference here in Obadiah to 'the house of Joseph' is undoubtedly a reference to the Northern Kingdom.

Israel (the Northern Kingdom) here called the 'House of Joseph' had been deported from her country by the Assyrians and has been largely forgotten by history. In that coming day of deliverance and victory they will join with the Southern Kingdom and be reunited as a combined nation to experience the blessing of the Lord. It would be

The End of a Nation

"the uniting of Judah and Israel who had been separated and enemies since the death of Solomon" (Hailey).

The united kingdom of Israel at that time will be all-consuming. In that day the 'house of Jacob' is described as 'a fire' and the 'house of Joseph' is described as 'a flame'. The nation is pictured therefore as a roaring fire, which consumes all before it. It is a powerful picture of total and absolute destruction and the fuel for that fire is the nation of Edom, namely the descendants of Esau, who are here described as 'the house of Esau'. Stubble tends to be dry and highly burnable. In late summer and early autumn farmers in arable areas tend to burn the stubble in the fields. Stubble is the base of the crops left in the ground when the harvesting is over. Edom is seen here as highly inflammable and being consumed and destroyed in the flames of Israel. So at that time Israel would enjoy victory, namely deliverance from the tyranny of Edom.

The result would be that Edom would be utterly consumed and 'there will be no survivors'. No one, absolutely no one would remain from 'the house of Esau'. This has been the recurring message throughout the prophecy of Obadiah. Here the message is reinforced with the direct word "The Lord has spoken". Let there be no doubt that what Obadiah has said will come to pass because the Lord has spoken it. God does not make thoughtless comments or make ill-advised statements. When God speaks it is with authority and the assurance that what He says will come to pass. Edom the cruel nation would be utterly consumed.

The cruelty of Edom was not an exaggeration. In A.D. 70 they joined in with the Roman soldiers of Emperor Titus and entered the city of Jerusalem, which had been under siege. Altogether there were 20,000 Edomites or Idumeans as they were called at that time. They turned on the Jews in what has been described 'as a mad career of slaughter'.

The Book of Obadiah

Josephus the ancient historian records that in one day they killed 8,500 Jews in the outer temple. They massacred priests and stamped on their bodies to defile them and then set about murdering the general population in large numbers and tortured those who escaped immediate death. It was the most appalling violence and most awful cruelty. We can also remember that Herod the Great was the monarch on the throne at Jerusalem when Jesus was born. It was he who received the wisemen and discovered that Christ would be born in Bethlehem. It was Herod who ordered the death of all the children aged two and under in the Bethlehem area. Herod was of Edomite descent and was well known for the most terrible cruelty. That was the nation of Edom and no wonder God's judgement was focused upon its people.

Edom's demise as a nation was a slow and steady decline. It began with the Chaldean invasion under Nebuchadnezzar who brought the nation into subjection; later Edom was invaded by powerful Arab tribes known as Nabataeans. They drove the Edomites out of their country and they settled to the west in an area of Southern Judah, which they had previously overrun when the Jews had been deported into captivity, and there they remained for about four hundred years.

Later the Edomites were subdued under the Maccabees. Judas Macabaeus defeated them in 164 B.C. and killed about 20,000 of them. John Hyrcanus who forced the nation to be circumcised and to accept (at least nominally) the Jewish religion intensified that subjection. He placed a Jewish governor over them. Later during the period of the Romans and despite the brief power of the Idumeans (the New Testament name for Edomites) under the Herods the Edomites gradually disappeared. They appear to have been absorbed into the Arab nations and their identity was totally lost.

Is there any application for us as individuals? Of course, there must be.

The End of a Nation

God does not desire or overlook the cruelty and injustice that people inflict on others. We as Christians are called upon to hate the things that the Lord hates and He hates cruel behaviour, injustice, selfishness, arrogance and all that is sinful. Therefore we should avoid these modes of behaviour in our own lives at all costs. We must wage serious and sustained war upon sin and the sinful urges that so easily arise in our hearts. We cannot be victorious over the temptations that afflict us unless we reach out for the strength of the Lord to help us. So each day we need to pray, in the words of the Lord's Prayer 'and lead us not into temptation, but deliver us from the evil one'. Likewise we need to remember that when Jesus was tempted by the Devil He fought the temptations with the words of Holy Scripture. A mind well stocked with the Word of God has a great defensive structure against the forces of temptation which we meet each day.

There may be times when we fall and sin against the Lord. We need not stay failed and defeated. The Bible says "if we confess our sins He is faithful and just to forgive us our sins and to cleanse us from all unrighteousness". (*1 John 1.9*) So when we fail we need to 'confess' that is to seriously be sorry for our sins and make no attempt to justify them or cover them. They need to be confessed, renounced and repented of and the Lord is able to clear our account and give us that fresh start we require to continue in fellowship with Him and serve Him in a full capacity.

The Book of Obadiah

Reading: Obadiah 19-21

"The inhabitants of the south shall possess the mountains of Esau, and the inhabitants of the Philistine lowland they shall possess the fields of Samaria. Benjamin shall possess Gilead. And the captives of this host of the children of Israel shall possess the land of the Canaanites as far as Zarephath. The captives of Jerusalem who are in Sepharad shall possess the cities of the South. Then saviours shall come to Mount Zion to judge the mountains of Esau. And the kingdom shall be the LORD's."

The message of this shortest book in the Old Testament has been directed at the nation of Edom. It announces the judgement of God against an arrogant and violent people, who directed so much of their venom at the nation of Israel. However, the focus of these final verses is the nation of Israel coming into the fullness of its inheritance with the blessing of the Lord upon them.

One of the great blessings when reading Holy Scripture is that God never forgets His people. They may have been invaded, besieged, deported and many killed. They may have been the objects of mockery and scorn, with their enemies seemingly invincibly strong and they as weak and insignificant. Yet God had never ever forgotten them and He would restore them fully to their land again. This needs to be constantly remembered as there continues to be economic, political and military disputes in the Holy Land. There will come a day when God will bring to fulfilment the words written by His prophets of old. As one commentator has written: "Here is a glimpse into Millenial days. Israel becomes the head of the nations and the instrument of rule for the reign of Christ." (Rudge)

The End of a Nation

We see in these closing words of Obadiah the full extent of Israel's influence and domination. The four points of the compass are used to describe Israel's inheritance.

1. Southward: there will be Israelites living in the south of the country, in the area of semi-desert south of the city of Hebron, known as the Negev. This was the area that David lived in when he was a fugitive, on the run from an acrimonious King Saul who wanted to kill him. Those Israelites will conquer and possess the area around the Dead Sea, including "the mountains of Esau".

2. Westward: this is where the Israelites will gain control over the Mediterranean coastal plain and the foothills that lie behind it. During most of the Old Testament period this area had been populated and controlled by the Philistines, who had been present since the twelfth century BC. The Philistines had been a strong military power, with well-built and fortified cities. They had been a constant thorn in Israel's side and had at times dominated the nation. At other times when Israel was strong, as in the reigns of David and Solomon, they had subdued the Philistines and restricted their power and influence. In a coming day all such power will be subdued.

3. Northward: here the influence of Israel will move to hills and mountains in the central and northern areas of the country. The people of Israel will dominate the mountains of Ephraim and Samaria. Presumably that influence and control will move into Galilee and Northern Palestine.

4. Eastward: here there is reference to one of the tribes of Israel, namely Benjamin. This was the tribe that was loyal to the throne of David and his descendants. This tribe, and this tribe alone, remained with Judah to form the Southern Kingdom with its capital city at

The Book of Obadiah

Jerusalem. It would seem that in that coming day when Israel possesses its full inheritance that Benjamin will expand its boundary beyond the River Jordan and onto the East Bank area of Gilead.

So the first verse in our reading defines an increased geographical area for the nation of Israel where they will exercise power, influence and control. The kingdom will have been restored to its furthest extent, but seems to principally deal with the Southern Kingdom, the restored Kingdom of Judah.

The next verse *(v.20)* appears to be the restoration of the Northern Kingdom, which had been deported and scattered so that no real knowledge had remained as to where they were dispersed. Thus Hailey comments: "The captives of Israel's host who had been carried away into lands throughout the world would not be forgotten. These would share in the redemption and the possessing of their rightful heritage."

Some of those exiles would return and possess the area of 'the Canaanites' and will occupy the land as far as Zarephath. This was the town that Elijah had once stayed in during a time of famine and drought in Israel. It was there that he stayed with a widow and her son, and they were kept alive miraculously by the constant provision of flour and oil. During that time the son died, but was raised to life by God in a miracle through the prophet Elijah. *(1 Kings 17)* This town was located to the north of Israel in the region of the cities of Tyre and Sidon. This area was sometimes known as Phoenicia, as it was that great seafaring people who inhabited that region. Today we know it as the coastal region of the nation of Lebanon. So Israel is envisaged as stretching to that area.

A second group of exiles are then mentioned as being originally from Jerusalem but had been deported to Sepharad. This place Sepharad is a

The End of a Nation

bit of a mystery and no one can be categorically sure where it is, though a number of suggestions have been made.

Firstly, some have concluded that this is a reference to Spain and there seems to be some rabbinical tradition to support this idea. This may be the reason why Spanish Jews are known as Sephardic Jews. This idea must seem unlikely, as no Jews had been deported to Spain in the days of Obadiah. However, this might have been a long-term prophetic statement that relates to dispersion yet to take place after the time of the prophet.

Secondly, the great Latin translator of the Bible named Jerome has made another suggestion. He considered the word to be an Assyrian word, meaning 'boundary'. Thus he took the view that this referred to a region of Assyria and this accords well with the known history of the Northern Kingdom. However, Jerome seemed to suggest that the region was the southern part of the Black Sea in the area, which today is known as the Bosphorus. This area would be located on the northern coast of what today is known as modern Turkey.

A third suggestion is that the name 'Sepharad' refers to the city of Sardis that was the ancient capital of the kingdom of Lyddia. That kingdom was located in Asia Minor, which today is modern Turkey. It was certainly true that in the first century there were many Jews in Asia Minor, as is witnessed by the visits to synagogues that the early missionaries, Paul and Barnabas made on their journeys.

The fourth suggestion is the most plausible and links to some extent with the second. This is an area of southwestern Media where the northern tribes of Israel were deported. In the words of Gaebelein: "The most likely identification, writes Archer, connects Sepharad with a district referred to in south-western Media mentioned in an

The Book of Obadiah

inscription of King Sargon of Assyria. It is well known that Sargon deported some of the ten tribes to the 'cities of the Medes' *(see **2 Kings 18.11**).* Therefore, this locality would have been very appropriate to mention in Obadiah's prediction." Certainly in ***Acts 2*** when people gathered in Jerusalem to celebrate the feast of Pentecost there were Jews from Media *(**Acts 2.9**)* and even into modern times there have been Jewish groups in this area in what today we call southern Iraq and Iran.

So though we cannot be categorical about the locality of this place, the weight of evidence would suggest that it was the kingdom of the Medes. Thus exiles from Sepharad would be part of the group that inhabited the cities of the south, namely the drier areas of the Negev, south of the city of Hebron.

So we see the geographical area of the newly emergent and triumphant people of God.

Local residents and returning exiles all have a part to play and will inhabit the area of what might be termed Greater Israel.

The prophecy ends with a powerful note of triumph and a contrast is made between Mount Zion and Mount Esau. This contrast in view of all that has gone before in this prophecy must be a deliberate finale. 'Saviours' or 'deliverers' will ascend onto Mount Zion. The idea of these 'saviours' finds an echo back to ***the book of Judges,*** when God raised up 'saviours' (known as 'judges') to deliver Israel from foreign invasion. They were warrior judges who with the help of the Lord and indwelt by His Spirit were able to win great victories and to drive the enemies of Israel out of the Promised Land. So in a local and restricted sense Obadiah is looking forward to earthly leaders who would lead Israel to victory over her enemies, and certainly there have been a

The End of a Nation

number of such individuals. However, "these 'saviours' are at best foreshadowings of the Saviour, who was yet to come in Obadiah's day and whose second and glorious appearing we are now awaiting." (Gaebelein)

These leaders will be there to defend Israel and punish Edom. They will move out from Mount Zion and 'judge' or 'govern' the mountain of Esau. Thus Edom is under the authority of these 'saviours' but ultimately that means they are under the authority of God. Thus Edom's closing vision is of justice carried out righteously and the worldwide dominion of the Lord bringing blessing for mankind. These deliverers will exercise authority in the name of the Lord, but ultimate sovereignty will be His alone.

The book closes with the words, "And the kingdom shall be the Lord's" *(v.21)*. "None of the prophets has a more exalted close than this. It looks forward to the words of Revelation: "The sovereignty of the world has come into the possession of our Lord and his Christ, and he will reign forever and ever." *(Revelation 11.15)* " The simple fact is that no human kingdom or empire endures for ever. Earthly sovereigns come and go. They hold responsibility and power for a time and are accountable for how they exercised that power, but no man-ruled empire or any nation of this world will endure forever. All will one day be merged into that eternal kingdom over which the Lord Jesus Christ will reign in solitary glory." (Gaebelein). The people of God have never doubted that God has always ruled as king, but every believer waits for that full expression and acknowledgement by everyone of His sovereign rule. One-day God's people shall rejoice when "the kingdom of the world has become the kingdom of our Lord and of his Christ, and he shall reign for ever and ever." *(Revelation 11.15)* In that day "every knee shall bow, of things in heaven, and things in earth and things under the earth, and every tongue shall confess that Jesus Christ

The Book of Obadiah

is Lord to the glory of God the Father." *(Philippians 2.10-11)* What a glorious prospect it is for each and every Christian to know that we are part of that Kingdom and will be with the Saviour forever.

So we come to the end of this shortest book of the Old Testament and it would be good to take a few moments just to reflect upon the lessons learnt from this writer who penned these words hundreds of years before the birth of Christ.

Firstly, we have noted that this is the shortest book in the Old Testament, but it is part of God's inspired Word. It would be easy to by-pass it and neglect its teaching and that would prove to be serious loss to our spiritual lives. It may not be easy to get into its context or application, but we have seen that detailed study produces rich dividends for our souls even from such a short book.

Secondly, we have seen the seriousness with which God views our inner attitude. The pride, arrogant boasting of Edom was an affront to the holiness of God and caused indignity to the people of God. God's punishment upon Edom was largely due to her pride. We must be careful to bring our ego into subjection and not ever become inflated with our own sense of worth. We may have a bright mind, good ideas, a logical approach, a strength of character, a strong and attractive physique, we may be successful in our business or our professional life and we may be financial well off and well endowed with this world's goods. Yet these things should be our servants and not our masters and so we need to exercise care in our attitude towards them and also in our attitude towards other people as a result of them. We must submit to the Lordship of Jesus Christ and serve Him with willing obedience for the glory of God.

Thirdly, if inward attitude is a cause for concern so is the outworking

The End of a Nation

of that attitude into character and behaviour. The wrong attitude can become the root of a great deal of wrong reactions, wrong words and wrong behaviour. The two are intimately linked. What we are in our thinking and attitude is reflected in our character and behaviour.

Fourthly, Obadiah clearly and unmistakably points out that God will bring severe judgement upon those who break His laws. Sinners will face punishment and no one will be able to accuse the Lord of unfairness or of injustice. His judgement will be seen to be absolutely fair. However, there is an escape from the awfulness of divine punishment and that is through the Saviour the Lord Jesus Christ. He came to earth to die on the cross at Calvary to take our sins and be punished for them. Through true repentance and genuine faith in the Saviour we can experience forgiveness and the wonderful joy of looking forward to Heaven.

Fifthly, we remind ourselves that the Lord always keeps his promises. In this prophecy the sure promise is that the nation of Edom would not continue to triumph and gloat over Israel. Instead "they shall be as though they had not been" *(v.16)*. This certainly came true and today we have no nation on earth named 'Edom', they are a lost nation and their cities lie abandoned and deserted. The prophecy of the Lord came true.

Sixthly, we must remember that this message was from the Lord and Obadiah is at pains to point out that the source of the message did not come form his own mind but through a vision from the Lord. That is always true and the message of the Gospel we proclaim today is not of human devising, but the result of divine wisdom and planning for the good of mankind.

Finally, God's people are encouraged to "possess their possessions".

The Book of Obadiah

That would be true for Israel, but is also true for Christians. We should enter into the good of the spiritual riches and treasure, which are available in Christ. Let's search for those treasures through the Bible, the Word of God. Let's appropriate those treasures through prayer and let's apply them into our daily lives by the power of the Spirit of God. What a wonderful blessing that is and glory is brought to the name of the Lord as a result.